DEVOTIONS

from the

"Bare-foot Pastor"

by Rev. Debbie Drost

Devotions from the "Bare-foot Pastor"

Copyright © 2015 by Rev. Debbie Drost

All rights reserved. This book or any portion thereof may not be reproduced or used in any manner whatsoever without the express written permission of the publisher except for the use of brief quotations in a book review.

First Edition.

Editor: Nicole Bailey at Proof Before You Publish
Cover Art: Kellie Dennis at Book Cover by Design

Dedication

This devotional book is dedicated to my Lord and Savior, Jesus Christ. I was only the vessel he used to speak to you. He laid it on my heart to send these "mid-week" devos in 2006. Many times I would write them, guided by his words, and think "Lord, that doesn't make any sense!" Our Lord knew exactly who needed to hear it. Thank you God for letting me send the blessings.

Love as God Loves

Love from the center of who you are; don't fake it. Run for dear life from evil; hold on for dear life to good. Be good friends who love deeply; practice playing second fiddle.
Romans 12:9-10 (The Message)

Praying over this scripture today, (because it takes me in a lot of different devotional directions), the first sentence kept sticking out.

Love from the center of who you are... What is in the center of who I am? My first and only answer to that; it is **God who is the center of who I am.**

So if **GOD** is the center of who I am, then I need to ***LOVE AS GOD LOVES.***

To love as God loves, we need to stay away from evil and hold on to the good that is around us. Some days that is really difficult.

I have a good friend in the ministry who felt compelled to **CONSTANTLY** remind me, "It's not about you." That is difficult to remember when you are as precious as I am. (See, it is with good reason he has to remind me.)

Playing second fiddle, helping others to shine for Christ, is a wonderful example of a good friend and disciple.

As Jesus went to the Cross, **he played "second fiddle"** when he put all of us first. He set the example of what it truly means to "**love deeply.**"

From the Heart

Each man should give what he has decided in his heart to give, not reluctantly or under compulsion, for God loves a cheerful giver.
2 Corinthians 9:7

Jesus wrote more about money and giving than almost any other subject in the Bible. It is one of the most difficult things to deal with within the Church and within our lives.

I love this scripture because it clarifies, to me, what God is saying to each and every one of us about giving.

Giving is decided between you and God. He knows where you are and he loves you where you are. Many times we feel ashamed or bad because we cannot give what others are giving, or that we cannot "Biblically live up to giving ten percent".

Please let me assure you that God is aware of your circumstances. **He knows** when you do give that you give what you can, and He knows whether you are giving with a *CHEERFUL HEART*.

Know also that where you are today with your giving is not where you will be a year, five years or ten years from now. Your life circumstances will change and God will continue to bless you every day because that is the kind of God we have.

Paul says in Philippians (in the revised Rev Deb version) that we are:

"Pressing on toward the Goal."

Inside and Out

God said to Moses, "I am who I am. The Great 'I AM'."

Exodus 3:14a

Mark Shultz sings a beautiful song called "I AM". Part of the song goes like this:

I AM the Spirit deep inside you…
I AM the Word upon your heart…
I AM the one who even knew you...
Before your birth...
Before you were...

Is God surrounding you today? Is He reminding you of who he is? Reminding you that **NO ONE** will **EVER KNOW** you as **HE KNOWS** you? **NO ONE** will **EVER LOVE** you as **HE LOVES** you?

Be excited today knowing that the **GREAT I AM** is that spirit within you, the Word on your heart, and the one who knows you inside out and loves you beyond understanding!

At a Price

You were bought at a price. Therefore honor God with your body.
1 Corinthians 6:20

What a powerful scripture to remind us what Jesus did for us.

He paid the price.

This past weekend I was at a Women of Faith Conference where Max Lucado was one of the speakers.

He made a reference to that price. He said that Jesus basically told God:

"Whatever the sentence is for the person that committed acts of violence-**place it on me**."

"Whatever the sentence is for the thief-**place it on me**."

"Whatever the sentence is for the man who committed sins against his own daughter-**place it on me**."

And in those few moments on the cross, before death took him… **God did**.

Therefore honor God with your body.

How are you honoring God with your body today? I don't mean taking care of it. We all know we have to do that.

I believe, today, that God wants us to use our bodies as a **LIGHT** for the lost, a word of **HOPE** for the one in darkness, and a **FRIEND** for the friendless.

Our bodies are "*Temples for the Holy Spirit*" (vs. 19), to be used for the greater good of the Kingdom. May your day be blessed with the opportunity to do so.

"Honor God with your body"

A God-Listening Heart

GOD appeared to Solomon in a dream: God said, "What can I give you? Ask."
1 Kings 3:5 (The Message)

Solomon could have asked for anything, but here is how he answered God.

"Here's what I want: Give me a God-listening heart so I can lead your people well, discerning the difference between good and evil. For who on their own is capable of leading your glorious people?"
1 Kings 3:9 (The Message)

What a powerful answer, and one that I echo in my own heart as a Pastor. Give me wisdom, Lord!!! Not a day goes by that leaders everywhere are not faced with discernment of some kind.

All the money and power in the world cannot replace God-given wisdom to know the difference between good and evil.

In all we do, let us pray for a God-listening heart.

The Finishing Touch

Today I have been in Galveston for the major part of the day. My son, Brent, had his yearly diabetic checkup with his diabetes specialist.

As I was driving home it occurred to me how awesome our God is. You know, when He made us, He did not spend much time on the essentials.

I mean, when you go to the doctor you don't have to have a special book that tells him where your particular **"innards"** are...

God created all our hearts in the same place, our kidneys in the same area, mouth, nose, eyes, **ALL THE SAME PLACE.**

What God had fun with was the paintbrush he used to give us that special touch.

The little touch that makes him smile when he sees us dance.

The touch that amuses him when he hears us laugh.

The touch that makes his heart warm when he hears us praise and worship him.

We were made to amuse our God -- some of us amuse him more than others.

As for me, I think he has a good ol' belly laugh when he watches me.

You see, it proves God has a great sense of humor.

Healed and Well

In Beth Moore's new book "Get Out Of That Pit", there is a conversation between her and her husband.

He asks her the question, "What do you think I would have been like? If all that hadn't happened? If I hadn't been so messed up and turned to so much sin. What do you think I might have been like?"

She said God gave her the words to say to him, "Honey, you're a much neater person *healed* than you would have been well."

I am humbled at how much God has **healed** me. I look back at the times in my life when I have been messed up and in the pit of sin. God's hand was there to lift me out of the pit and **heal** me.

The amazing part is that he does not just **heal** us. He **blesses** us more than we are ever worthy of being blessed.

Are you in a pit today? Are you having difficulty seeing a way out? **Look up**...there is a hand right above you and that hand belongs to the great Physician.

Healing is only seconds away.

Hold Me to It

The Webster's dictionary defines the word *accountable* as "explainable".

Here at my church, I am in an Emmaus Reunion group. **It is an accountability group**. We meet every Wednesday. I am not always there. I wish I could say it is because of my "pastoral duties". The truth is, it is part of my laziness!!!

We ask these questions of each other:
   When this past week, did you feel closest to Christ?
   At what moment this week did you feel you responded to God's call to be a disciple?
   When was your faith tested this week through failure?

This group holds me accountable **for and to my faith**. I also join in holding each of them accountable for their faith.

The truth is, the answers are not always pretty and they have a certain "look" when they know I am making stuff up. Ha!

One day, beyond any doubt, we will stand before our God and HE will hold us accountable for our faith. It will not matter who buys the groceries, who mows the grass, or who makes the most money.

It will matter if your faith is strong enough to get you to the final stand! So, get started early… Be a part of an accountability group (Bible Study, Emmaus, SS class, etc.).

We need to be held accountable...as painful as it is at times. We need to help hold our brothers and sisters in Christ accountable.

Always With Us

Are there times in your life when you are still "amazed" by the work of the Holy Spirit?

Today I went into my office to get some work done before I had to head to the several meetings related to our annual summer camp.

I received a phone call shortly after I got to my office that one of our members was dying, (he has been sick for a while) and his family wanted me to get there as soon as possible.

I dropped what I was doing and went to be with them. I stayed with them as long as I could before I had to get to the camp meeting. I had forms that had to be turned in today for our kids to go to camp.

I went to the one meeting to visit with the other camp directors on lunch break. After about a 2-hour camp meeting, I sit here typing this, amazed at the work of the Holy Spirit today.

I have gone from a place of work, to a place surrounded by death, to a place surrounded by 3000 people voting on God's work, to a place of breaking bread with camp volunteers, to now a place of reflection.

The Holy Spirit of God is all around us wherever we go. He will protect us, give us words to say, and energy to do what is asked of us.

Finding God

I have a dear friend who was involved in a horrific car accident a few years ago. We were told at the time that he would not make it -- **but he did.** Then he was told he would never walk -- **but he does**. Because of the injuries to his head, he was told he would never be able to live a "normal" life.

Actually, the doctors were right there. He does not live a "normal" life. He lives a very "abnormal" life **because he spends his time and monetary gifts helping Churches come in to the technology age**. He is using the life God has given him back...to help others find their way to God.

He has been installing new computers, which he bought and brought down to the Church I serve, and trying to update us on computer language. He laughs because he can tell when he loses us because our eyes glaze over in the explanation of megabytes, mini bytes and other stuff.

Jesus tells us that all we have to do to find him is to seek with our whole heart. No special wiring, no special training, no special language. A desire to be whole, to be forgiven, and to yearn to live an eternal life with him is all we need.

Praise God for people like my friend, who helps others find their way to God, and

We ESPECIALLY praise our God who makes it very easy to find him.

Unexpected Rest

Today is an unexpected blessing. A SABBATH day in the middle of the week!

As I look out the window here at home, at the lake, there is ice hanging from the deck chairs and roofline.

I have caught up on my Bible Study lessons, worked on the Church Transformation information that our Church is involved in, and will begin soon to work on a funeral I will do tomorrow.

Before that, I think a good nap is in order.

"Come to me, all you who are weary and burdened, and I will give you rest."
Matthew 11:28

Have you been given a Sabbath day today? UNEXPECTEDLY? If so, email me back and let me know how you have spent this time God has given you to rest.

The Thorns of Life

This morning, with a sermon to prepare for Sunday, **(yes, I do know it is Friday!!!)** I decided to go work in my little flower garden. Spend some time with God where it all began. EXCEPT, I knew there were no weeds, at least not as many as I had "where it all began".

I had rescued this rose from the "dead and dying" tray from Home Depot late this summer. It has bloomed continually since I planted it and it has the most wonderful smell.

I cut it back today, but saved the beautiful rose that was on it. As I went to enjoy the smell of it, I realized it had some pretty big thorns. Well, those thorns were big enough to see and skirt around. But the stem was lined with those almost "hair-like" thorns. I could not get to the rose without touching some of the small sharp thorns. But, AAAHHH the smell was worth it.

Sounds a lot like our Christian life, doesn't it?

The rose (Jesus) is so worth getting to.

We know in this life we will be traveling through some thorns. Some will be big enough for us to "skirt around". We can see them. We can even remove them pretty easily. But it is the little ones in this life that attack our faith, that get under our skin before we know it.

You know the ones. The little thorns that take some digging with a needle and tweezers. The ones we decide to just leave there till they grow out, **but they never do.**

Keep your eyes fixed on the rose. Jesus does not need a needle and tweezers to remove the sins from our life. In fact, sometimes he can do it quite painlessly.

The Talent You Gave Me

I received a wooden cross for Christmas from a dear friend of mine. It had an unusual saying in the middle.

"When I stand before God at the end of my life, I would hope that I would have not a single bit of talent left and could say, 'I used everything you gave me'." Erma Bombeck

I have decided **THAT** should be my New Year's resolution. How powerful is that?

To be able to stand before God and hear him say, *"What did you do with what I gave you?"* I believe he will ask us that.

And for us to be able to say, "*I USED EVERYTHING YOU GAVE ME.*"

Some reading this are well on their way to being able to answer that way.

Some of us better get started.

How is it with your TALENT gauge this morning?

Hills and Valleys

One of my assignments at my time at Lon Morris (theology school) was to go back **10 years** in my church history and chart the growth in certain areas of membership.

I had only been appointed at the church that I served at during that time for a few months, so it was a little bit of a challenge for me.

I can't express the relief I felt in wrapping that project up. I looked back on the hills and valleys of the church over the past 10 years. There it was, all on paper, numbers, but not feelings.

What was not on paper was the reason for the hills and valleys.

The paper did not show the pain or joy that the congregation went through during those hills and valleys. The times they prayed to "just get through". It did not show WHY someone left. Or WHY someone joined, the tears over the deaths, or the tears over the baptisms.

If you had to chart the last 10 years of your spiritual growth, what would the chart show? Would it show more hills? Or would the valleys seem really deep?

Could you pick out the Hand of God or would there be more times that left you wondering **where the Hand of God was?**

Every now and then it is good to look back to see where we have been. But the real JOY is looking at where we are going.

The only thing that I really want to get out of **MY PAST 10 YEARS** is the courage to walk forward, knowing without a doubt that my **GOD** got me through those 10 and **HE IS STILL SMILING. (I think maybe even laughing some.) :-)**

Learning for a Lifetime

One of my dearest friends is deaf. She is one of the most remarkable women I know. She is going to school to become an interpreter for the deaf community. She signs for the Praise and Worship service at her church and it is **one of the most beautiful things to watch**. She has been very patient with me in teaching me some sign language.

One of my wishes is that God would just sprinkle the sign language in me and I would not have to try and learn it at my age. (No feedback please!)

At the Emmaus Walk a few weeks ago, we were blessed to have another God Gifted Sister in Christ who signs for her church. **She was just beautiful to watch.**

So I decided that it was time for me to really learn to communicate in this most graceful language. I really want to surprise my friend, so don't tell her I am starting to practice again.

Being a Christian means having to learn a new language. For some of us, that new language is extremely hard to learn.

The Language of Love, Forgiveness, Grace and Mercy takes a lifetime of PRACTICE.

We are so blessed to have a TEACHER who is there for us at any time of the day or night.

As we learn how to share the language with others **it is THE most beautiful thing to watch**.

Revelation and the Art of Asking

^{30} When he was at the table with them, he took bread, gave thanks, broke it and began to give it to them. ^{31} Then their eyes were opened and they recognized him.

Luke 24:30-31a

What is your bread today? What is it that opens your eyes to be able to recognize the risen Christ?

Is it your children? Your spouse? Reading scripture? Maybe it is through your prayer life. A homeless person? The sick or dying?

Maybe you have never seen the risen Christ.

Do you want to? **There is no big secret to it.** All you have to do is ask. God loves to make himself known to you. He is not trying to hide from you. He is just waiting for you to ask him.

At our Walk to Emmaus this past weekend, I had several people come to me and tell me that Christ had revealed himself to them. They had seen the risen Christ because they had asked him to make himself known to them and he did.

God loves you...and he wants you to have no doubt of who or where he is

All you have to do is ASK...

Miracles Do Happen

MIRACLES DO HAPPEN....

Almost 5 years ago I went on a spiritual journey. I attended a **Walk to Emmaus**. It was a weekend that not only strengthened my spiritual journey, but it put a bond between me and God that has sustained me through some incredibly difficult times.

Between the beautiful spirit God placed in the Lay Leader and the love for God that the Spiritual Director had on my walk, they instilled such a desire for me to always be a part of this incredible ministry.

I have since worked walks every year, in a servant role. My heart's desire was to be a part of the Spiritual Team. A desire I thought could never happen because of some "technicalities" in the denomination I worked for.

More than that, I have sinned beyond any hope of ever being placed in such a place of importance in God's world.

Then God calls me to work Emmaus Women's Walk #38. I am one of the Spiritual Directors for this walk. Five years after taking that first walk.

I am the one God wants to spread his ministry. He needs those of us that have sinned, those of us that have felt the heat from the gates of Hell. Those of us that have been on our knees, face down, in tears and with broken hearts.

He needs those of us that have been lifted up and repaired by the almighty Hand of God. He does not need the perfect people that know nothing of his grace and mercy and forgiveness.

In God's world, **I am a walking MIRACLE**. Just as the blind was made to see, the lepers were cleansed, the lame made to walk.

I can see! I am cleansed! And I leave tomorrow to share the light burning in me with the Women on Walk #38.

Here's Your Sign

I received a phone call from my son a few weeks ago. He had been to visit us (i.e. get clothes washed, eat dinner, and get MONEY) one afternoon and on his way back to College Station he came across a Church sign with a message on it that he thought was pretty cool.

"What is missing…CH__ __CH?"

He was so excited to tell me that he saw this. (Hooked on Phonics paid off.) He figured out all on his own that it was **U R**! Ha! I asked him if he thought God was trying to tell him something.

God puts so many messages in front of us every day to help show us the way. Many times they are so small that we pass right by them without every catching them. We pass by and say, "That was pretty cool. I wonder who that was meant for?"

Keep your eyes open, dear fellow Christians, God is "emailing you, calling you, putting big letters up on billboards for you".

As one of my favorite comedians says –

"HERE'S YOUR SIGN"

Choices

A few years back, we were praying about our son Brent, and his choice of life ministry. He lived in College Station at the time and was going to EMT school in preparation for starting at the Fireman's academy.

The thought of my son (then 19) running into burning buildings to rescue babies, kids, teenagers, adults and the elderly was frightening for me. I want them to be rescued, but I didn't want my son to be hurt in the process. I can't even imagine how he might feel when the day comes that he comes in contact with the one he could not save in time. My heart hurts at just the thought of it.

Can you hear God saying, **"BEEN THERE, DONE THAT! *MY SON* DOES THIS EVERY DAY AND YES, MY HEART HURTS FOR THE ONES WHO *CHOOSE* NOT TO BE SAVED IN TIME."**

I have a curling iron that turns into *SATAN* every time it gets close to my neck or forehead. A burn is a hurt that is unexplainable. Every time I get a little burn, I think, this is what it is like for all those who do not know Jesus Christ as their Savior, except an eternity of it.

I love the scripture in Joshua that says, "Choose this day whom you will serve. As for me and my house, we will serve the Lord."

The same goes for eternity, CHOOSE THIS DAY WHICH SECTION YOU WOULD LIKE TO BE SEATED IN:

SMOKING OR NON-SMOKING

The Weed and Root

Good *God* morning to everyone.

I have plenty of *"MARY"* things to do today, but the *"MARTHA"* in me just could not look at the weeds in my flowerbeds one more minute.

I have a medium-size flowerbed. You would think that I could do better at keeping the weeds out, but to tell you the truth, it is depressing to keep pulling the same weeds out again and again. Some days I think I will just forget it and let the weeds take over.

Then I look at the beautiful roses and bougainvillea and lantana that are all in beautiful colors and I know I have to get my lazy-self up and pull the weeds. ***ONE MORE TIME!***

I know part of the problem is I don't always pull the weed *AND ROOT* up. So it grows back.

Much like our sin comes back. We think that if we cut the top off of our sin, it makes us GOOD CHRISTIANS. But God is looking for us to allow him to *PULL THE SIN OUT FROM THE ROOT.*

In my human nature, I would think that God would get very tired of watching us wrestle with our sins ourselves. He knows the root is still in us and will grow again if we do not let him pull it out for good.

Why doesn't he just say forget it and let the sin take us over?

Because He looks at us and sees the beautiful colors of the rose, bougainvillea and lantana growing in us.

Faith is not an action! It is a response!

A few days ago I received an e-mail asking for prayers for one of our members' family. It seems his niece, age 25 and 7 months pregnant, had died in her sleep. I know the struggle I have over this, so I can only imagine the faith struggle the family is going through today.

They ask for prayers for their faith to be strong enough to get them through this. All of us that have been through "The Valley of the Shadow of Death" and made it through know that our faith **in the one and powerful God** is the only thing that brought us through.

We were discussing this in our Bible Study this morning. **How strong does our faith have to be to pull us through the darkness?**

ALL of us at some point go through unexplainable tragedies. That is the way of this world we are passing through.

Don't wait for the dark times to see how strong your faith is. **START NOW!** Before tragedy hits!

Get involved. Bible studies, workshops, serving in the church or community.

Being in fellowship with Christian friends and family, reaching out and working on your relationship with Christ.

Get familiar with being the hands and heart of God...that way when the darkness comes, you will know the feel of **HIS HAND** as he takes **YOUR HAND** to walk through it with you.

Your Breathtaking View

As I sit here at home, at my husband's computer this morning, I am watching the sun come up over the lake and **the view is breathtaking.**

Yesterday, I was at the hospital visiting some friends' newest granddaughter. She was born Wednesday and as I held her and looked into that precious little girl's face, **the view was breathtaking.**

Can you imagine what the Garden of Eden must have looked like? I was born in Hawaii and have been back several times since adulthood. I figure that is close to how Eden must have looked, only a billion times better.

How blessed and loved we are by a God that, even though he had to banish Adam and Eve from there, would show us a little bit of Eden every day. In a sunrise, or a sunset we see him. In the face of a newborn baby, in the love on the face of our children and spouse we see God's love.

For the person reading this and needing to know, YES!

You are forgiven.

Through the grace and powerful love of our Lord and Savior, you are forgiven.

Remember...

"LIFE IS NOT MEASURED BY THE NUMBER OF BREATHS WE TAKE, BUT BY THE MOMENTS THAT TAKE OUR BREATH AWAY."

Take a moment today and find **the breathtaking view** God planned just for you.

That was Easy

Many of you know that I have a son that has type 1 diabetes. He was diagnosed when he was 11. He has to take close to 5 shots a day.

We got a letter a few weeks ago from our insurance company that needed confirmation of his enrollment in college last spring for his coverage to continue.

It was a simple piece of paper that needed to be circled and signed by the college.

I stopped there on Monday and was informed they could not do it without Brent's permission. He had to sign this blue piece of paper giving ME permission to get someone to circle and sign my white piece of paper.

Through nothing short of a miracle, I got my son to sign this blue piece of paper Monday night.

Tuesday morning I went to the college and presented them with both my papers. The lady smiled and said it takes twenty-four hours to have someone CIRCLE my paper and that I could stop back by on Wednesday and pick it up. Which I did. (**##!*)

What would we do if God required this much time and effort for us to receive Salvation? Would we do it? Not many would.

What is even more amazing is that many don't today and we are not even required to get out of our car, make three stops, and face people that pushed our peace button.

God has made spending eternity with him as easy as asking him to come into our lives and be our Lord and Savior.

OUR GOD IS TRULY AN AWESOME GOD

God's Wash Cycle

Today I am working from home because I have the very heavy burden of loving on my 1-year-old grandson for the next 3 days while his family is floating on a river somewhere.

I am trying to "multi-task" while he is playing with all my pots and pans and ***rubber spatulas***.

I grabbed one of the 10 loads of clothes I needed to wash and as I was putting one of them in, I began to think about how many times I have washed these clothes over the last year or two.

No matter how hard I try, it is impossible to keep them clean. You might be able to wear them a time or two, but eventually they are going to have to go through the wash cycle.

I began to see what God's wash cycle must look like. No matter how hard we try, it is impossible for us Christians to stay clean. Eventually we say something or do something that sends us right back to God's wash cycle.

Last night our worship committee went through boxes of old clothes that were just too stained to clean.

Some of you reading this devotion this morning may be feeling like you are too stained to be cleaned. Your sins are too many and too dark. And even worse, is the one person who believes their stain (sin) is small and does not need to be cleaned.

May you find true cleansing through the mighty Hand of God this day.

All we are required to do for cleansing is ASK.

The Juggling Act

I am honored to share this devotion from my daughter.

A couple of weeks ago our Pastor did a sermon series on supporting the church through your prayers, presence, gifts and services.

In the sermon on the giving of your services, I felt God touch my heart as he has so many times before. We were challenged to take on a new study or become part of a new group or take on a new project in the church this next year.

About that time, my ***SWEET*** husband looked over at me and held up one finger, reminding me that I should not "overdo" my time and become a "less-than-sweet me."

I knew that God was calling me to sing in the new service, start a disciple class, help rev up the Emmaus community and start a new adult Sunday school class.

All of this has been on my heart for a long time. I can honestly say that I am not stressed out about any of these things. ***NOT because I am superwoman and eat stress for breakfast...*** But because I know that God will do these things ***through me*** and He will do them in **His time.**

I am allowing myself to fully trust him and I will just sit in the crowd and watch in amazement as God, the Lord of Lords and King of Kings uses a lowly sinner, such as me, to build up his kingdom on this earth.

Understand that when you are asked to do something in a church, you need to take the time to ***pray about it and commune with God.*** Ask him if this is your ministry that you were created for, or if this is someone else's ministry that you will be taking away if you accept.

Let God lead and guide you to choose your ministries in the church and outside of the church. Be willing to step out of your comfort zone and ***TRUST that God will take over.***

THEN, sit back and watch the show, for if you fully trust him, you will no longer be in control.

Not by Yourself

Many of you know that my favorite scripture is found in John Chapter 15. (The Vine and the Branches).

Part of Vs. 4 says...Remain in me, and I will remain in you. NO branch can bear fruit by itself:

This week is Vacation Bible School, as it is at many churches this week. We are having ours in the evening. Every afternoon about three, I can feel myself starting to moan... (As I am sure most of the devoted servants are!)

I am ready for the couch and a cold Diet Coke, not trying to gear myself up for another four-plus hours of singing songs and dancing around like I physically won't be limping tomorrow.

By six that night this place is rocking with people and children, and I begin to feel all the excitement and energy from ***my fellow Christians.***

We not only gain our power and energy from God, but ***we feed off of each other***. Our Christian brothers and sisters sharing the faith and love of God.

As we first remain in God, ***we need to then remain in each other.*** We don't have to bear fruit alone.

In fact, the scripture goes on to tell us that by remaining in God (and each other) we will bear ***MUCH fruit.***

Part like the Red Sea

When I am walking with Clayton, my 11-month-old grandson, he loves to bend over and watch our shadow move with us.

It reminds me of how God moves with us. How we are never without him. We cannot outrun him, out-jump him, out-hide him, and yes, even out-love him.

I love to listen to KSBJ. Along with half of the world it seems. It is great to listen to a radio station all day that is dedicated to serving God.

One of their sayings is, **"Don't tell God how big your troubles are... Tell your troubles how big your GOD is."**

Sometimes when we look ahead, our troubles seem so huge. So overwhelming! We stand frozen in fear and indecision on going forward.

But when you really close your eyes and begin to concentrate on telling your troubles how big your God is, it is an amazing thing how the "red sea" of troubles part and there becomes an opening for you to not only walk through, but to dance through.

The Blessing Gives You a Choice

I realized (again) the other day that ***ALL*** blessings in this life come with a price.

Monday morning I walked out and looked at my flower garden that I have neglected for a few days, acting like the wicked witch in the Wizard of Oz.

I'm melting... I'm melting...

Then the rain began to fall. I looked toward the heavens and gave God thanks for helping with my laziness. I got dressed and headed into downtown Houston for a week of meetings.

It was not long before the blessing I felt that morning for the raindrops, turned into travelers' nightmare. It was a high price to pay for all the flooding and wrecks on the side of the roads.

What a blessing it is to move into a brand new and beautiful Church facility, to welcome a new Pastor or a new child. Some of the prices though, are a feeling of losing that "family church closeness", losing a Pastor you have come to love, and not knowing if the "new Pastor" will be all you want him/her to be.

And raising that child with so much love and having to come to a time when you have to give him/her to God because of the direction they chose in life after they grew up.

Our Salvation came with a high price, not only through the death of our Lord and Savior, but a price to us, to get up...step out...move forward to proclaim the word...and to sow the seeds of love to a hurting world.

The blessing? It gives you a choice.

**"WHERE WILL YOU SPEND ETERNITY?
SMOKING OR NON-SMOKING?"**

A Little More Time

⁶Then he told this parable: "A man had a fig tree, planted in his vineyard, and he went to look for fruit on it, but did not find any. ⁷So he said to the man who took care of the vineyard, 'For three years now I've been coming to look for fruit on this fig tree and haven't found any. Cut it down! Why should it use up the soil?' ⁸'Sir,' the man replied, 'leave it alone for one more year, and I'll dig around it and fertilize it. ⁹If it bears fruit next year, fine! If not, then cut it down."

Luke 13:6-9

Have you grown tired of waiting for your "fig tree" to bear fruit? (i.e. Your prayers to be answered.)

Are you ready to just cut your losses and move on to something else? Why should you spend any more time on these prayers (use up the soil) when you cannot see any fruit bearing possibilities coming from them?

Don't give up...God answers ALL prayers... Take the advice of the caretaker of the vineyard, "Give it some more time". Stay connected to God and when it's time for your answers to come, they will come and bear more fruit than your eyes and heart can take in.

Gracious Changes

Last week I was sitting in a hospital waiting room with one of my members as his wife was having surgery. I wanted to share with you a part of an article I read in a magazine.

"I need help...a few weeks ago a strange woman moved into my home. No one invited her and I cannot get rid of her. She has somehow taken over every mirror in my home. Her face is wrinkled and her hair is gray. MY skin has always been baby smooth and my hair has always been thick and blonde. WHO IS THIS WOMAN???

She is changing everything around my house... I went to get my 2-inch high heels out of my closet and they had all been replaced with some kind of shoe with SAS on the side...

I reached for my Cosmopolitan magazine and all I could find was these AARP magazines."

WHO IS THIS WOMAN...??

These temples God gave us to serve him change, sometimes for the better, sometimes NOT.

Taking care of them is much harder with every passing year.

Always remember...

God loves the baby smooth skin and blonde haired woman and he loves the "gracious changes" that come to all of us in time.

Being the Change

I was called into ministry in 2002. I was not sure where God was calling me but I was "pretty sure" it wasn't preaching. You've just got to love God's sense of humor. What could God ever want with a Mississippi barefoot preacher?

And a woman to boot!

Five years ago I obeyed Christ and stepped out of the mainstream denominational church and through His guidance and twelve friends, we opened the doors to Living Water Church of Spring. We rented a type of "storefront" building with around 3200 sq. feet.

Last month, we moved into our new facility. We now have a 7600 sq. foot church building sitting on 3 acres of land. Those 12 friends have turned into 120 families, everyone still my friends.

I could spend the next 20 pages filling you in on my doubts, fears, and miracles over the last 5 years but that is water under the imaginary bridge.

Within the last few months I have had several women contact me, asking to, "Tell my story?" What story, I say to myself?

Who am I (hey Moses, how you doing today?) that they would think I had something to share?

My Church gives me an allowance of $1,000 to attend a leadership conference of my choice every year. The last 3 years I have attended different ones all led by men in the ministry who have paved the way.

This year I wanted to find one that could help me in my leadership role. Would you like to know how many I found for women being called into ministry and leadership? I am sure your first guess was correct.

None.

So, I did what I usually do and complained to God.

"Hey, God. How am I supposed to keep up my strength and excitement if I have nothing out there that can speak to my calling? I love Women of Faith and Girls Night Out events. They speak to my brokenness and resurrection. But, what about my 'calling into leadership and ministry'?"

Where can I learn to break through my fears and obstacles as a leader in a man's dominated world? I don't want to take over for me, I just want to fulfill my own calling.

"So, (yep, still talking to God) if there is nothing out there for us women (Mississippi remember), what do I do? Where do we find workshops and worship time and speakers that can help us move forward in ministry?"

You become one!

And with that simple answer from God **"The Ignite Group"** has been formed.

Looking Back

God allowed me to close some doors on my past recently. There were some things that I have held onto for forty-give years. Those were finally released to a bright and wonderful life that God has given me.

I love how our God so wants to lead us to a powerful place to honor him but He can't bring us full throttle because we are holding on to the past and "wondering" about the "but what if's" in our past.

A few conversations this weekend from the McDonald clan (my brothers & sister):

In the middle of the gym floor being filled with people, when the MC asked for everyone that had been coached by Coach Mac (my brother) to come stand beside him.

My sister: "Wow...that is so amazing that he is so loved and touched so many people."

Me: "Yes, he has certainly bloomed where God planted him."

My sister: "Who would have thought it?" (Remember we are his sisters!)

Me: "Well, if you were to come to Texas, to our church, everyone there thinks I am an angel."

My sister: "You've got to be kidding." (Gotta love family, My sister really is my biggest fan.)

Later that evening when we were all gathered around Tony's living room and he was sitting at the table with 2 of his friends that stopped by.

My oldest brother: "My sister, see the one in the pink?" The other two guys nod their heads.

My oldest brother: "She is a preacher." (insert humble heart here... mine)

God: Let the past hurts and questions GO! If I did not need you or have greater things than you or anyone could imagine, I would have let you stay where you were and never would have born powerful fruit.

I realize I could have been HAPPY if I remained in Florida (where I grew up), but the JOY that can only come through God's plans for any of us, would never have been found.

> Thank you God for the prayers
> that are always answered.
>
> And especially for those that are
> answered with a gentle NO.

Religion or Relationship?

I have always had a huge heart for the Sacrament of Holy Communion. Different Churches celebrate it in different ways.

When God called me to step out, and further UP...to lead his people at the church I pastor, I had an opportunity to put my God-given priorities in line.

At the church I pastor, we celebrate Holy Communion every Sunday in both services. I believe in becoming one with God every chance we get so that we can do all things through him.

I also believe with all my heart in the scripture in Luke 24:31. It was not until "The breaking of the bread that their eyes were open." Why would I ever deny anyone the chance to see Jesus, if that is the way he intended to reveal himself to someone?

I believe Churches who only allow certain people to take the Holy Sacrament of Communion will have to answer for that someday.

That being said, at the church I pastor, Communion is open to all, 2 years old, or 102!

> Hence the time of the God Moment"S".

Sunday as I was giving Communion, we had a new family with a young boy around 10. When he came up to receive, I said the same thing I say to all children who have not been through Confirmation. "Jesus loves you very much."

The boy just looked at me with his eyebrows raised and said, "Me? Does he really love me?" My heart just broke.

Three people behind him became one of our members. He is only about 9 years old. I told him, "Jesus loves you very much." He looked straight into my eyes and said, "He loves YOU very much too Pastor Deb."

My eyes and heart were open to Jesus through the breaking of the bread.

> What I would have missed if I were more into the Religion instead of the Relationship!

Can These Bones Live?

[The Valley of Dry Bones] The hand of the Lord was on me, and he brought me out by the Spirit of the Lord and set me in the middle of a valley; it was full of bones. He led me back and forth among them, and I saw a great many bones on the floor of the valley, bones that were very dry. He asked me, "Son of man, can these bones live?" I said, "Sovereign Lord, you alone know."

Ezekiel 37:1-14

Have you ever felt this scripture was meant just for you? No matter how hard you try, life resembles a valley of dry bones?

Yesterday, you were in the middle of "the Spirit of the Lord" and PHOOF! You now find yourself in the middle of a valley of "dry bones".

Where did the excitement of getting up and going to work go? What happened to the JOY of being around others?

Why does the question "What am I meant to do" or "Is this all there is" keep ringing in your head?

Why have my prayers not been answered when all around me "others" are celebrating their prayers coming to fruition?

Any direction I step right now is surrounded by dry bones. Anywhere is better than this valley I am in, but how do I get out of it?

God says, "Answer my question first and then I will answer all of yours."

What question??

"Son of man, can these bones live?"

What is your answer?

When God Closes a Door

I get these emails from this Christian card company and the one I received yesterday packed a powerful punch for me.

I mean really, how many times have you heard the saying, "When God Closes a Door, He Opens a Window"? Hundreds? Yeah, me too.

I started to just gloss over it when I realized it said something different. I have attached it for you if you want to save it to remind you later.

The saying started out the same, "When God closes a door" then it changed. "Stop banging on it! Trust that whatever is behind it is not meant for you."

Do you ever feel sometimes like your life is a scene from the Wizard of Oz?

You know, when the guard tells Dorothy and them to go away and he slams the door? They all just sit by the door and lament. For them, the door reopened and they were meant to go in. But what about us?

How long have you been waiting for a door to reopen?

How many times have you beat on it and begged God to open the door, thinking there is something gentle and powerful that you are meant to have waiting on the other side?

When in all reality what lies behind that door is a darkness you could never imagine just waiting to consume you.

It's a new year with lots of adventure laid out for you by the one and only Almighty God.

We can put all our trust in the one that closed the door and sees behind it, or we can continue to bang on it till our knuckles bleed and our voice is raw.

How much time have you wasted banging on a door that will not open ever again when the party is one faith step away?

Join God for the best year ever.

Don't waste another minute of this year looking back at a closed door.

Meet and Greet Time

Even though we are not a new church any longer, we have just moved into a new building in a new location.

I have been a Pastor for about twelve years now and this survey (or one just like it) I have included with this devotional is and has always been a topic of Pastors' conversation. As Pastors we have (or should have) one thing on our minds, and that is to make sure Jesus has control of our hearts.

That's the reason it is best not to ask your Pastor questions about meetings or what is next week bringing on Sunday mornings. If they are any kind of Pastor they have gone into Jesus mode and that is where they should stay. Talking about Church politics or asking for minutes from the last meeting will bring your Pastor in and out of Jesus mode. If that happens, the instant result is "The sermon seemed a little off today".

The "meet and greet time" in Church services is a fine line for most churches. I know how hard those few minutes are on a visitor. I see it with the visitors in our church. At some point, all of us were that first visitor standing there, wishing this part of the service was over.

My first thought to my worship team was to tell them to call everyone back to their seats.

The other side of the coin is the precious moments of laughter and the sounds of hugs. Yes, I can hear hugs in our church. It sounds like the sound you make when you just finished the best Thanksgiving meal ever.

This is one of the best parts of our church service. My prayer for any visitor is to notice that this is a church FAMILY that they truly want to belong to. They want to feel the love and presence of the Lord Jesus Christ that lives and breathes life into everyone that enters the living room of God.

The only reason anyone, visitor or member, should get up on a Sunday morning, get dressed and leave their living room, is to seek God and to Worship him in HIS living room.

If a visitor feels the presence of Christ in any church it won't be long till that "meet and greet time" will be one of their favorite times too.

Jesus says in Jeremiah 29:13, You *will seek me and find me when you search for me with all your heart.*

Unstopping the Flow

Ever feel like the "well has run dry"?

That place in you that is like our Living Water Church scripture...**"Whoever believes in me, as the scriptures have said, rivers of living water will flow from within them." John 7:38**

I have been writing the mid-week devos since 2002. Have I run dry at times? Lots. Have I felt like no one is reading or getting anything from them? Lots. Do I think God is through with this ministry and ready to let that stream dry up? Obviously not, so here goes.

I love watching Duck Dynasty.

One of my favorite episodes is when Phil and his family head out to the creek and find the dag-nabbit beavers have built a house of sticks over the water and stopped it from flowing down the creek.

Satan's favorite place to build a house of sticks is over the living water within our souls.

It looks a lot like the beaver house...except our sticks have names on them, pressure, bills, no time, sadness, loneliness, anger.

A stick of dynamite is what Phil and his family uses to blast the beaver house apart and get the creek going again.

I don't recommend a stick of dynamite to blow up Satan's house on our living water but we have something much more powerful and much easier to use.

It is just one word, according to the scripture. BELIEVE! Believe that your God is stronger and mightier than anything Satan could ever pile against you and then...

Be amazed at the flow of the living water running again through your thirsty soul.

The Visiting Preacher

I was texting my son, Brent, this morning.

We had just opened our new church building and the smell of that newness sat all around me as I waited to hear back from him.

He asked me how our second Sunday in the new church went.

I told him it was good but I kinda felt like a "visiting preacher".

Know what he said?

He said, "You are a visiting preacher Mom, it's God's house."

Always a nice reminder that one – they do come back (Brent) and two – God's house is His. You and I are beloved, welcomed guests. Next time we enter into the Church let's ask that host of the home what He would have of us and open ourselves up for his presence to wrap around us fully.

Jesus, Me and the Duck

I have been told I need to get back to walking, but I hate exercise. So I decided not to look at it as exercise but a time to meet Jesus and walk with him. Just me and him. I put on my praise and worship music and started steppin'! So far it has been five days.

This morning, Jesus was having me remember how he called me in many of the just me and him moments.

We were walking around the lake here in my subdivision. Trees so green it hurts your eyes just looking at them. The sky so blue that it could have only been painted by the one that walked with me.

We were coming up to a duck standing by the walkway. Jesus laid it on my heart to "look at the duck". Since I am so precious I already knew what he wanted me to look at. It was a Mallard and one of the most colorful ducks.

I said, "Yes, it is beautiful." The next second the duck turned his head and looked straight at me.

   Then... the duck started shaking his whole back end. Just like a dog wagging his tail when he sees his master.
   I busted out laughing. It really was a God Moment.

Four Years at the Church I Pastor

Wow! This Sunday Living Water Church ("LWC") of Spring will celebrate 4 years of church life. We opened God's living room at the church I pastor the first Sunday in June, 2010.

This will be the last year in the building we are in. Ground has been broken for the new building in the place God chose for us to do his ministry in. All of us, and those praying for us that belong to other church homes all over the country, stand in AWE at the power of God in this place.

LWC is a place for "misfits". We use that term with a lot of love at LWC. The name works for us because we just don't quite fit into the box of rules.

We are a people that just want to worship God. We are able to feel comfortable singing loud with no "singing lessons".

We are able to raise our hands in worship, or not, and not worry what people think.

We EXPECT AND INVITE God to show up and show off in his living room.

And HE has not failed to do so in the 4 great years and we already know he is working at the new location.

It is really so simple to feel church instead of doing church at Living Water.

I believe anyone at LWC will tell you that when man-made rules are left at the door of the church and God-given love is breathed throughout, "worship" takes on a more powerful experience.

We don't believe we are a "non-denomination" church...We believe we are ALL denominations, open to all hearts that are looking for a place that their

"JOY can be restored."

Decisions

Decision. That one word can bring up a level of "stress" like nothing else. For the biggest part of our lives, the decisions we make are pretty simple.

What's for supper? (I really dislike this one. How about you?)

What should I wear today?

Which way should I go to work to stay out of traffic? (Oh wait, there is no easy way.)

Sometimes it gets to a more difficult level.

Should I have the treatments or just wait?

Do I need to show "tough love" or wait?

There is always the life changing decisions.

Do I accept Jesus as my Lord and Savior?

Do I spend eternity in a mansion or in Hell?

Do I live a life that Jesus has set up for me?

Do I continue to struggle through what the world tells me I should do?

Then again...Some decisions are just a "no brainer".

Share with God what decision you are facing today.

Restoring JOY to Your Marriage

A while back, God laid it on my heart to do a marriage study. As with most things God tells us to do ... I tried to get out of it.

I am no expert in marriage and at this late date in my life I had no desire to become one. I did not want to take time to study and put together something that would pass as a study for couples.

There are two things to ALWAYS REMEMBER WHEN DEALING WITH GOD.

One, if it is something He really wants. He will not let up on you!

Two, the only requirement to His request is SURRENDER. I may not know how to lead a couples study but God sure does!

Last night we had our first class. Friends, there were 13 couples that showed up. None of them had any idea what direction the study would go, (remember who they have for a Pastor).

The men had no idea if they were walking into a "man bashing" just for being men. The women had no idea if they were walking into a room of guilt for not being a Proverbs 31 Woman.

And yet...I had twenty-six people sitting in God's living room, waiting to see what God wanted from them.

Do you know what He wanted?

He wanted them to remember, to recall, to feel to the depths of their souls, the JOY of being married to the one they said "Yes" to.

In this class, we are not allowed to bring any negativity. No blame! No pain! (There are actually people that get paid big bucks to deal with those things).

We laughed. We cried out with ahhh's.

I know there were conversations in bedrooms last night that said:

> "I didn't know you felt that way about me."

> "I forgot for a few moments (years) that it was your blue eyes that turned me on first time I saw you."

> "Do you really believe the strength I bring into our marriage is Christ?"

I realized that there are so many studies out there on how to have a better, richer, less painful marriage.

This world beats marriages to death.

It shoves the two of you so far from that moment you stood before God, looked into each other's eyes with all the JOY in the world, and pledged the two of you to become one with Christ.

In this study we are remembering the JOY and being willing to let God restore it.

Our church has a "hash tag" that reads, "Come Have Your Joy Restored."

No one can steal your JOY. It is a gift from God. All Satan can do is cover it up with doubt and pain.

Our God can restore all. Won't you let him?

Being a Mom

"They" say that the last words you speak on your deathbed are the ones that are straight from the heart.

Here is what Jesus said on his, in John 19:26-27, *When Jesus saw his Mother and the disciple whom he loved standing nearby, he said to his Mother "Woman, behold your son!" 27 Then he said to the disciple, "Behold, your Mother!"*

Some of his last few spoken words were to make sure his Mother was taken care of.

There is no other relationship that has such a special place in the hearts of women as that of their children.

What is the best thing about being a mom? (Hold on we will talk about that one in a minute.)

What is the worst thing about being a mom? Guilt! Plain and simple.

      Guilt: Not washing everything that touches the floor with the second child as the first.

Sending them off to school after a yelling match at breakfast.

Working away from home to make sure they get the "things" they need.

They choose a wrong path...so it had to be something I did wrong.

I couldn't "FIX" that huge boo-boo.

I should have been a better mom.

I should have spent more time with them.

I should have chosen their baseball game instead of cleaning house.

I should have, I should have, I should have.

All of that guilt is crippling.

Given to you as a special gift from the one that wants to spend eternity with you. He has prepared a place for you. Right slap dab in the middle of the "smoking section".

My relationship with my mother was never easy. She carried things from her past into our relationship and I was never going to be released from the mistake she made.

I had a choice though. God is a great God that way. I could choose to have that same relationship with my kids or I could choose to let God give me a new heart...

I knew the only thing I would like to have on my tombstone…"She was a child of God and she was a good Mom."

Want to know why I can relate to the guilt? As with you, I have done all of those things above (and many more).

NOW, some of the best things about being a mom?

> Those little pictures on your icebox.

> Huge heartfelt smiles when pulling out ornaments from years past.

> A hug from tiny arms or really big arms. (You get the point, this one could go FOREVER).

God does not, repeat, does NOT give us a burden of guilt.

It is going to hit us because Satan wants it to, but like in Mississippi where we build shotgun houses, your guilt has access to a back door -- straight through. Make sure that door is open because if not, all that guilt is building up in a very tight, stuffy, hurtful room.

Jesus made this relationship special, who are we to load it down with "I should have's"?

Where are you on that road?

Luke 24:13-35 tells one of my favorite stories in the New Testament, the Walk to Emmaus. It begins with a simple reflection that sets the stage for the reader and draws into question the importance of this story. Pastor Deb unpacked this narrative beautifully and I've added footnotes from her sermon below.

"Now on that same day..." What day? In looking just before those words, one will note that it is the resurrection day -- Easter Sunday still. Christ rose from the grave and showed himself to the women and then we move quickly to this story on the road to Emmaus.

It shows how important we are to the Lord and how our concerns and troubles are of great concern to Him. Of all things He could be doing in those moments, He took time to walk along with two troubled disciples and open their eyes to His very presence.

Where are you on that road?

Are you troubled and in need of an encounter with Christ? Have the troubles of your situation or circumstance weighed you down so much that you fail to recognize Him because the wind and the waves are all but swallowing you?

Are you a little further down the path (in the story) and in need of Jesus Himself to open the scriptures to you and speak truth into your life? Open your Bible and be blessed by who God is and the realization that you might have skewed him to be a harsh owner or a demanding father. You couldn't be more wrong.

Are you standing at the door of a decision or along life's ebbs and flows and hearing the soft knock to open up and let him in for the first time, or even deeper than He is already? Don't let him stand outside and knock, but like the two disciples on the road to Emmaus -- invite him in to stay.

Are you seated at the table, assured of your relationship and living in the spirit each day and simply need to see him once again in the breaking of the bread? Prepare your heart and mind to receive His goodness and come expecting.

Where are you on that road, because I assure you, you are somewhere. Find your starting location today and move another step closer. Close your eyes and breathe in deep as your heart burns within you at the very recognition of your Creator and King.

Ahhh... but the end is the best. When Christ left them they got up and returned to Jerusalem to tell the story that Christ was indeed risen. When is the last time you told your story? Surely your ashes have been turned into beauty because of who God is, not who we are or what we've ever done to deserve it. It was in the telling of the story over and over by the various disciples that you and I belong to a body of believers known as the Church.

Don't keep the greatest cure known to humanity for all that ails us and leaves us awake at night. Share your story and remember how Christ has made himself known to you on your own personal walk to Emmaus.

Time Out

So it seems I am having one of "those days".

You know the ones, where even a blade of grass causes you to grumble. Nothing big, just grumpy.

If the lady at the grocery store check-out needs a smile, she should look to the one behind me.

What if someone wants some help? I am pretty sure this "well" is dry!

Can't get the jar open? Car door catches your finger? Knife slips and cuts your thumb?

O.K. you get the picture.

What we don't get is that someone is always watching our Christian responses to things. Always!

If you are having a hard time today with "Joy Overflowing" then get out of the way of others as much as possible.

Take a time out. As a kid that was a bad thing, but as an Adult Christian it is a necessity.

Christ makes it very clear on how our "Un-Christian" attitude can cause others to stumble.

Causing to Stumble

"If anyone causes one of these little ones—those who believe in me—to stumble, it would be better for them to have a large millstone hung around their neck and to be drowned in the depths of the sea.
Matthew 18:6

Maybe before the millstone around the neck, we could just take a "time out".

A Sense of Humor

Over a week ago I was eating a Hershey bar with almonds. I know that is nothing remarkable! But, this particular Hershey bar had an almond hull in it and my back tooth wanted to be friends with it. Half the tooth decided to leave with its new best friend. (And you thought Jesus was good at speaking in Parables.)

I thought it would be OK since there was no pain with it. The one thing we can count on in a situation like that is the pain does not stay away forever.

To make a long story longer, I ended up in the dentist chair yesterday.

Conversation with the new dentist helper:

Her: So you are a Pastor?

Me: (here we go) I smile and nod my head

Her: I have only known one other woman Pastor (No doubt her religion at this point).

Me: Yep. God has a funny sense of humor.

Her: I know a lot about God and Love him dearly but I am not sure you could say he has a "sense of humor".

Me: (Oh Lord, don't let her touch this tooth!)

The tooth took a John the Baptist death. It ended up being a wisdom tooth I didn't know I still had.

As I was leaving with a mouth full of gauze, the helper said to me after giving me instructions what to do and not to do.

Her: And above all of that, don't SNEEZE. It could cause you to get a dry socket. Have a great evening!

How can she not see GOD HAS A SENSE OF HUMOR!

Bigger Than Us

¹⁹Consequently, you are no longer foreigners and strangers, but fellow citizens with God's people and also members of his household, ²⁰Built on the foundation of the apostles and prophets, with Christ Jesus himself as the chief cornerstone. ²¹In him the whole building is joined together and rises to become a holy temple in the Lord. ²²And in him you too are being built together to become a dwelling in which God lives by his Spirit.

Ephesians 2:19-22 19

I stand in amazement still. I am humbled still.

Three years ago this Sunday we opened the doors to a new living room for God.

Today, two of Christ's disciples representing the church will meet with contractors to begin the process of building a "dwelling" in which God lives by his Spirit.

In the human world it is foolishness to buy land and start building after three years of ministry. Well, it wouldn't be if we had a few millionaires in our congregation (we don't, do we?)

We are a congregation of hard-working, God-loving people who put our nickels together every Sunday and make sure our Worship to God is first and foremost.

When we began, I told our congregation that in many denominational churches, the question of you being "loyal" to that church is always asked when you join.

At the church I pastor, we only ask you to be loyal to God. If you make God, as we have, the Cornerstone, everything else will flow as it should.

My concerns about leading a church of twelve (which by the Grace of God is in the 170's now) was relieved when God told me I just needed to surrender this vessel I walk around in.

Even though this vessel is bigger than it was three years ago (hahaha) so is my GOD.

God blessed the Church in the book of Acts as the twelve started out. The Holy Spirit came upon them IN THE BEGINNING just as he did us.

I can't tell you how powerfully humbling it is to be a part of something so much bigger than us. To be able to look back and see that through obedience and love, WE helped Christ bring a church building into being that will still be standing and loving people long after we are gone.

Community

As I was walking around the house this morning, I was asking God to lay something on my heart to send out for the Mid Week.

Psalms 52 was given to me. Now, I know some of the Psalms by heart but "52" is not one of them.

I started to read it and it is all about Why do you boast of evil, and your tongue plots destruction;

I thought "wow Lord..."

It wasn't until vs 8 that I understood what He wanted.

Psalms 52: 8-9

⁸But I am like an olive tree
flourishing in the house of God;
I trust in God's unfailing love
for ever and ever.
⁹For what you have done I will always praise you
in the presence of your faithful people
And I will hope in your name,
for your name is good.

No matter what is happening in this world: the destruction, evil plans, innocent deaths,

We have to be in community with other faithful people.

We have to continue to have HOPE in the plans the Lord has for us.

We have to be the olive tree and reach out to those who are in need right now.

No matter what YOU are going through right now. I would imagine the precious people in Oklahoma would give anything to trade places. Trust in God's Unfailing LOVE for you.

Don't forget to PRAISE GOD for what HE has done and is doing in YOUR life right now.

Communion

While they were eating, Jesus took bread, gave thanks and broke it, and gave it to his disciples, saying, "Take and eat; this is my body." Then he took the cup, gave thanks and offered it to them, saying, "Drink from it, all of you. This is my blood of the covenant, which is poured out for many for the forgiveness of sins."
Matthew 26: 26-28

At the church I pastor, we take communion every Sunday. We also take it on special occasions, as tonight.

We also make sure that at ANY meeting at the church I pastor, we set a seat for Christ. The bread and juice very visible in case any of us forget what we are there for and who we are serving.

We all receive Jesus in many ways...through his word...through deeds we do...

But when we take the bread and the juice, which has been blessed to become the body and blood of Jesus, we truly become one with him.

As the body and blood is taken within our own bodies, we become stronger.

Jesus can do miracles with only a small amount taken in. It travels through every pore, every blood vessel, and every fiber of our being.

Jesus and the disciples shared communion in the "upper room" a long time ago.

When we take Holy Communion today, if we allow it to happen, we are taken into an upper room of our own. A place where just you and Jesus are together.

As you leave the upper room, Jesus goes with you, living and breathing in you.

Holy Communion is a precious gift to us. Never take it for granted and never take it without feeling it.

Slow down, take the moment that the bread and juice becomes one with you and give THANKS to the Holy One that believes you are worthy of his spirit living in you.

In the Name of the Father, Son and Holy Ghost.

Seek Him

Anyone having trouble locating God in the midst of your struggles?

Are you wondering why He has not stepped in and put an end to the nagging decisions you are having to make?

Why He has not answered you when you cry out?

Why does EVERYONE but YOU seem to have their lives together?

One of my favorite scriptures comes from Jeremiah 29. Most of you would immediately think of the scripture in vs. 11 (For I know the plans I have for you).

BUT in my world, it is Jeremiah 29:13 that brings me understanding of the questions that plague us in the first of this Mid Week.

You will seek me and find me when you seek me with all your heart.

Jeremiah 29:13

Don't try to find the answers to your questions in your MIND.

If you are like me you will wander around there forever without getting answers. (no jokes please. I already know what an empty place it is up in my mind…)

Open your HEART today for your answers.

It is in your HEART where God lives and breathes and WAITS.

The Time in Between

It is amazing how different the world looks just turning your head from the left to the right.

This morning I was watching all the camp kids dance and sing, getting everything ready for their day of hot weather and serving "the least of these".

You could not help but have a happy heart watching them.

Turning my head to the right and the "heart smile" turned to sadness as a hearse drove up to the front door of the church and family members gathered to bury a loved one.

How fast time slips away.

Those kids on the left did not sense the pain on the right and they shouldn't have.

From the left to the right.

How have we managed the precious time in between?

Eggs are Like Christians

I am serving in the kitchen here this week, and this morning we were cracking some "yard eggs" someone brought us. Of course someone cracked one and it had blood in it. I had to throw it all out with a disgusted shudder! The man next to me said, "Don't like to see that, huh?"

I said, "You would think it wouldn't bother me since I am from Mississippi."

He said, "You're from Mississippi?"

I nodded yes.

He said, "You sure have straight white teeth to be from Mississippi!"

What I wouldn't have given to still have that partial front tooth I had for so many years (I have an implant now).

How great would it have been to be able to pull it out and go "You mean like THIS?"

Sometimes you just have to take a compliment and move on!

Eggs are a lot like Christians.

We all need to go through the light before we can be worthy of being used.

Love to all

The Scales of Justice

Our Church, has been looking for a bigger place to grow and bring others into the relationship with Christ.

We have been looking for a while now with no results.

On my path to work every day, I pass a Mexican restaurant that has closed its doors and it was for sale for a long time. (No, that's not our new place.)

As I was driving by a few weeks ago, I noticed someone had bought it. I thought, "Oh! That's nice!"

A few days later there was a huge sign in front advertising for help. The help they need is women who are willing to serve tables in bikinis. We have a new bikini bar coming in.

Now, I don't care about the "Bikini Bar". God will do as he wishes.

My Problem????

House of Worship where many will find a way to the Lord.

Bikini Bar! (I have no response to that.)

Why does the scale of justice always seem twice as hard on us?

How Precious Are You????

Well, that's a silly question to ask me (for those of you that know me, it is my umbrella word to describe myself). I remember a time when I was about 15 and my family went on a shopping trip to Pensacola (I was raised in Milton, Florida) to find me a prom dress.

We had a rare treat to go to a restaurant to eat before the shopping. After eating, my sister and I went to the ladies room before we left.

I had worn my prettiest dress and just knew I could get no more precious than what I was seeing in the mirror as I left the ladies room.

Well, how great it was when I saw that everyone in the restaurant admired the "preciousness" in me too. Everyone was looking at me and smiling.

It was not until I was walking in front of my family to the car that they informed me my dress got hung up in the back (ladies you know what I am talking about)!!!!

It is amazing how fast "precious" can turn into THE MOST EMBARASSING MOMENT OF MY 15-YEAR-OLD LIFE (really maybe EVER).

YOU are PRECIOUS in the sight of Jesus. What does that statement mean to you and your life?

Favorite "Weather"

What beautiful weather we have been having the last few days. Many of you know that Roy and I just came back from a cruise. I was able to rest and "think" a lot. The wind was constantly blowing (sometimes you could not walk straight because of it).

It did not bother me because my favorite "weather" is the wind. I love how it feels when it blows around me. I don't care whether it is cold, warm, strong or mild. I love any kind of wind.

On the boat, I began to think how things we love can be dangerous to us if we aren't careful. The sun was bright and strong in the sky, but it was hard to tell the amount of heat it was pouring down on me because the wind was cool off the water. I turned my face toward the wind and enjoyed how it felt and did not realize the danger it was masking in the way of a sunburn.

We have to be constantly aware of our surroundings, even when we are in a place we love to be. The only protection we truly have that is safe, is our God.

Share with God your favorite "weather" and why that is.

Jesus Calms the Storm

This Devo is from my sister in faith, Laura Olsen

23 Then he got into the boat and his disciples followed him. 24Suddenly a furious storm came up on the lake, so that the waves swept over the boat. But Jesus was sleeping. 25The disciples went and woke him, saying, "Lord, save us! We're going to drown!" 26He replied, "You of little faith, why are you so afraid?" Then he got up and rebuked the winds and the waves, and it was completely calm. 27The men were amazed and asked, "What kind of man is this? Even the winds and the waves obey him!"
Matthew 8:23-27

I'm sitting here waiting for my friend to meet me. It's like a little piece of heaven is here on earth today. The sky is a beautiful shade of blue with fluffy white clouds playing in the air. A breeze is blowing -- teasing my hair and the trees. I lean back and look up. A tall pine tree is swaying and bending almost in time to the beautiful music I hear playing. I feel the breezes in my life -- tossing me about -- teasing and testing my faith. Will this breeze turn into a storm? There was such a storm that tossed me about, bent me to the ground and left pieces of me lying around. I thought I had split in half like some of the trees do sometimes, but God was not finished with me. He had not left me alone. I found out he had barely begun on me.

By his grace, he bent me to the ground and brought me back up again. I see the old pieces of me lying around on the ground. The pieces of worry, fear and mistrust were left behind. Like bark off a tree, the control I wanted to have blew off me. Jesus touched my soul and gave me life. Just as the pine popped back upright, he brought me back upright. My soul healed, the Lord has claimed my life. He will never leave in the storm. I may sway and bend, but I will not break. He is my strength and my life is his. He has rescued me and poured his love over me. His sacrifice allows me to have the breezes and the storms in my life. His sacrifice has shown me how to trust him and leave the fear and worry to him. His hand is always there, reaching down to pull me, to pull all of us, up from the ground and up from our storm.

Will you break or will you reach up for the hand of Jesus?

Waiting...

The only thing more aggravating than the word...is the deed.

This is one of the hardest things in life to do. Especially if you are "waiting" on an answer from God.

If you are waiting in line, in a doctor's office, or in traffic, you pretty much know it will be a while but the answer to that wait is within reach.

Waiting on God is a faith issue only. At 5:00 the doctor's office is going to close, at 5:00 God is still silent.

There are some BIG issues I am currently "waiting" on God to put light into the darkness for me, as many of you are.

I am tired of waiting. Anyone out there with me? Many people think those of us that have answered a higher calling (Pastor) have a direct connection to God -- you know, the "God phone". Like Batman and the bat phone.

As much as I wish it were true, it's not. We have to "wait" like everyone else. The blessing is, I know I am in some great company.

Even King David felt our pain.

Wait for the Lord. Be strong and don't lose hope. Wait for the Lord.
Psalm 27:14 14

Let's all do it together.
Let's hold spiritual hands and be strong together.

Imprinted Words

Hey everyone! I hope your day is going great!!

I was preparing for my women's Bible Study tonight and the topic is going to be on temptation – how we deal with it when we come up against it.

The two characters we're looking at are Eve and Christ. Eve accepted the lies of the great deceiver, but Jesus used weapons to fight against those lies.

In digging a bit deeper into that same line of thinking, I want to (once again) encourage you to pick up your Bible – it is called the "LIVING word" for a reason.

Jesus used scripture to combat the devil, and to teach the disciples, and to rebuke the Pharisees, the list could go on and on…

He used scripture because he knew it. Notice something, did he say, "In Isaiah 25:11… or In Malachi 1:7…" Did he quote the actual scripture or did he just speak the truth of its message?

Being able to deliver the message and explain its meaning is so much more important than knowing exactly where to find it.

Read your Bible and keep a notepad next to you – write down those things that you think, "Hmmm. There is a nugget of wisdom. There is a verse that answers Joe Bob's question. There is a phrase that will give comfort to my sister in need."

Or even better yet – "There is a verse that I can use against myself to remind ME that God sees something in me that I can't begin to comprehend. Today I'll repeat this verse and choose to believe what God sees in me, instead of what I see in myself."

Miracles Come in Cans

Miracles come in CANS....

I was listening to Joyce Meyers yesterday and of course when she said that, I gave all my attention to the show.

What was she talking about? Miracles come in CANS? Like a can of peas? Just open it up and pour it out?

At first I was like, "Ok, I am not watching you no more!" God might catch me and then I would be in real trouble!

But as usual, things are never what they seem. The show was on having the courage to step out in faith. Believing in yourself through the power of God.

I can do all things through Him who strengthens me.
Philippians 4:13

So, how are your "cans" this morning?

Are you struggling with something in your life that makes you feel like you "can't"?

You can't take that job?

You can't speak out?

You can't teach that class?

God is asking us today to open our CANS... Believe in yourself and the power HE gives you.

Don't let Satan tell you what you CAN'T do...

The ALMIGHTY GOD...TELLS YOU THAT YOU CAN! UNLEASH YOUR MIRACLE!

ABOUT THE AUTHOR

Rev Deb is the founding Pastor of Living Water Church of Spring, Texas. Started 5 years ago, the All-Denominational church just completed construction on their new facilities.

She is the Mother of a daughter, Laurie, that empowers her with courage and strength and a Son, Brent, who teaches her to slow down and enjoy the greatest treasures God gives anyone, which is family. It helps that she is married to her best friend, Roy, and has 3 perfect grandchildren.

My church family is the greatest cast of misfits God has ever assembled. This is truly the best time of my life.

Made in the USA
Columbia, SC
20 September 2018